BATTLES
THAT CHANGED THE WORLD

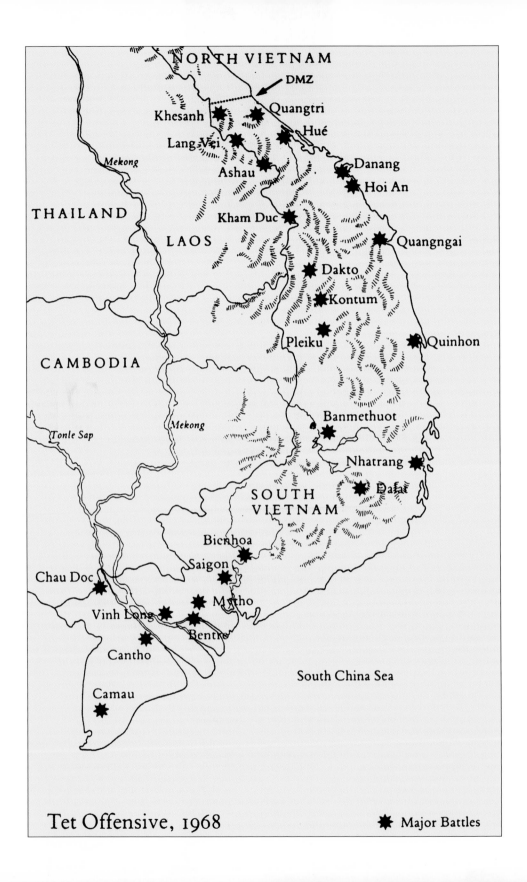

NORTH VIETNAM

DMZ

Khesanh   Quangtri
Lang Vei   Hué
Ashau   Danang
            Hoi An
THAILAND
            Kham Duc
LAOS   Quangngai
                Dakto
                Kontum
CAMBODIA   Pleiku   Quinhon

            Banmethuot

            Nhatrang
            SOUTH   Dalat
            VIETNAM

            Bienhoa
Chau Doc   Saigon
Vinh Long   Mytho
            Bentre
Cantho   South China Sea
Camau

Mekong
Mekong
Tonle Sap

Tet Offensive, 1968   ✹ Major Battles

TET OFFENSIVE

RICHARD WORTH

CHELSEA HOUSE PUBLISHERS
PHILADELPHIA

COVER: These U.S. Marines in South Vietnam advanced on the citadel of Hue City during fierce fighting for control of the city.

FRONTIS: This map shows the locations of the Tet Offensive's major battles in South Vietnam in 1968.

CHELSEA HOUSE PUBLISHERS

EDITOR IN CHIEF Sally Cheney
DIRECTOR OF PRODUCTION Kim Shinners
CREATIVE MANAGER Takeshi Takahashi
MANUFACTURING MANAGER Diann Grasse

STAFF FOR TET OFFENSIVE

EDITOR Lee Marcott
PICTURE RESEARCHER Patricia Burns
PRODUCTION ASSISTANT Jaimie Winkler
COVER AND SERIES DESIGNER Keith Trego
LAYOUT 21st Century Publishing and Communications, Inc.

http://www.chelseahouse.com

First Printing

1 3 5 7 9 8 6 4 2

Library of Congress Cataloging-in-Publication Data

Worth, Richard.
   Tet offensive / Richard Worth.
      p. cm. — (Battles that changed the world)
Summary: Details the pivotal battle of the Vietnam War.
Includes bibliographical references and index.
   ISBN 0-7910-6688-6 (hardcover) — ISBN 0-7910-7167-7 (pbk.)
   1. Tet Offensive, 1968—Juvenile literature. 2. Vietnamese Conflict, 1961–1975—
Campaigns.—Juvenile literature. [1. Tet Offensive, 1968. 2. Vietnamese Conflict,
1961–1975—Campaigns.] I. Title. II. Series.
DS557.8.T4 W67 2002
959.704'34—dc21

                                                              2002004475

CONTENTS

Lyndon Johnson was sworn in as president on November 22, 1963, following the assassination of President John F. Kennedy. Mrs. Johnson (left) and Mrs. Kennedy witnessed the oath in the cabin of the presidential plane.

President Johnson's Decision

"**A**ll I have I would have given gladly not to be standing here today," President Lyndon Johnson told a grieving Congress five days after the death of President John F. Kennedy in Dallas, Texas. During the sorrow and uncertainty that flooded over the United States following Kennedy's assassination on November 22, 1963, President Johnson proved himself to be a strong, calming presence to soothe a troubled nation. Johnson's leadership skills had been honed over many years in politics, as a congressman and later a senator from Texas, Senate majority leader, and finally vice president of the United States. Now tragedy had thrust him to the very summit of power. And Johnson wanted to be more than just a caretaker president holding America together until the next election, which was still a year away. He hoped to distinguish himself as a great president.

Over the next months, the president initiated a flood of domestic legislation that Washington had not seen since the days of Franklin Roosevelt's New Deal in the dark days of the Great Depression. Johnson spearheaded a massive Civil Rights act, which gave African Americans equal access to education and jobs. The president launched the War on Poverty, aimed at providing job training and employment opportunities for America's poorest citizens. Finally, he announced the beginning of his Great Society, a vast package of reforms that included free Medicare health insurance for the nation's elderly, extensive aid to education, a federal Head Start program for preschool children, and enormous financial assistance to improve urban housing. By the time he was elected to a full term as president in November 1964, Johnson had shown Americans that he was a dynamic, forceful leader.

But looming over President Johnson's impressive legislative agenda was a problem thousands of miles away that would eventually threaten his entire presidency— Vietnam. As the president told the distinguished journalist Walter Lippmann, "This is a commitment that I inherited. I don't like it, but how can I pull out?" Johnson's predecessors, presidents Kennedy and Dwight Eisenhower, had sent American advisers to South Vietnam to help support a weak regime against the attacks by the Communist government in the north. Gradually, President Johnson escalated the war by bombing the north in 1964. Early in 1965, when American advisers were attacked at their barracks in Pleiku, Johnson retaliated with more bombing. He also began sending combat battalions of marines to South Vietnam.

By mid-1965, 60,000 American troops had been sent to South Vietnam. Their numbers grew to 383,000 by the end of 1966 and would increase even more. From the outset,

President Johnson had harbored serious reservations about becoming too involved in Vietnam. He was afraid the war would become like quicksand, trapping all of America's resources. Yet he also believed that American security around the world required him to halt the forces of communism in Southeast Asia. At first, the president tried to carry forward both the war in Vietnam and the Great Society at home. But the costs put too great a strain on the economy. Gradually, he was forced to scale back his domestic programs to pursue the war.

At home, President Johnson faced increasing protests, especially from many young people who were being drafted into the war. They saw no reason to leave America to fight and die for a country thousands of miles away. African-American leaders, who had supported President Johnson's Great Society, realized that it was being abandoned in favor of fighting a war. In 1967 the Reverend Martin Luther King Jr. spoke at an enormous peace demonstration in New York, denouncing the Vietnam War.

As President Johnson faced mounting opposition at home, in Vietnam the war was not going according to plan. Communist Vietcong guerillas, supported by the regime in North Vietnam, proved much tougher than the American military leaders had ever imagined. The Communists did not crack under pressure from the powerful U.S. war machine. Johnson and his advisers were already beginning to realize that they could not defeat the enemy. Yet the president was not prepared to leave in shame. He saw the attacks by the Communist north as "a vicious and illegal aggression," and promised the American soldiers that their sacrifice there would not be in vain. "We shall never let you down," he told them in 1966, "nor your fighting comrades, nor the 15 million people of Vietnam . . . who are counting on us to show here—here in Vietnam—that aggression doesn't pay, and that aggression can't succeed."

Martin Luther King Jr. addressed a crowd of protesters against the Vietnam War on April 15, 1967, in New York City.

By the end of 1967, the war had reached a stalemate. Neither the Communists, nor the army of South Vietnam, with the help of the Americans, were winning the war. Indeed, there seemed to be no end in sight to the conflict. Polls were showing that Americans, who at first had supported the president, had now turned against him. They thought the war had become far too costly, especially in the face of more pressing problems at home. By June 1967, fully two-thirds of Americans said they had lost faith in President Johnson's ability to lead the country. They also mistrusted their government, which Americans believed, was not telling them the truth about the real situation in Vietnam. While the reporters covering the war were writing that it had reached a stalemate, President Johnson and his advisers were still publicly saying that the war could be won. But many of the American officers on the ground in Vietnam knew better—the war was not going their way.

President Johnson was expected to run for reelection in 1968. But he was challenged by a leader who was advocating peace efforts, Democratic Senator Eugene McCarthy of Oregon. In the first Democratic primary, held in New Hampshire in March, McCarthy almost beat the president. No one had expected such a result. But with his approval ratings at about 35 percent, the president realized that he had lost the confidence of a majority of Americans.

On March 31, he spoke to the American people about the course of the war in Vietnam and reaffirmed his commitment to stop the bombing of North Vietnam and open peace talks. Finally, at the end of his speech, President Johnson added: "I have concluded that I should not permit the Presidency to become involved in the partisan divisions that are developing in this political year. Accordingly, I shall not seek, and I will not accept, the nomination of my party for another term as your President."

The nation was stunned. But Lyndon Johnson had decided that only by taking himself out of politics could he be seen as an honest negotiator who was only interested in ending the war.

A major event had brought President Johnson to this decision. It was the impact of a decisive military campaign that had just ended on the battlefields of Vietnam—the Tet Offensive. The campaign had provided strength to the peace protests and led other Democrats to challenge Johnson's leadership. Tet had finally convinced the president that military victory in Vietnam was impossible.

Land of Conflict

Workers are shown harvesting tea in Indochina in the 1930s.

The story of the Tet Offensive began many centuries earlier in the history of Vietnam. Located in Indochina, historians have described Vietnam as a long, narrow bamboo pole with a basket of rice on either end. One basket in the north is the Red River Delta, where the city of Hanoi is located. Running southward is a peninsula bounded by the China Sea on the east and a range of mountains on the west. In the south lies the second rice basket formed by the Mekong River Delta. In this delta lies another major city of Vietnam. Once called Saigon, it is now known as Ho Chi Minh City.

For 1,000 years, beginning about 100 B.C., Vietnam was part of

China. The Chinese tried to modernize the country. They built canals in the Red River Delta to reduce the amount of flooding that occurred each year during the summer monsoon season. The Chinese also built roads, improved the Vietnamese harbors, and introduced the principles of Confucianism. Confucius was a philosopher who developed a set of principles to guide Chinese society as well as the government. Public officials, known as mandarins, followed the guidelines of Confucius in governing China and Vietnam. The Chinese also introduced the religion of Buddhism into Vietnam. Buddhist monks brought the teachings of Siddhārtha Gautama Buddha, who emphasized the importance of spirituality and selflessness.

The Vietnamese were never happy under Chinese rule, however, principally because the conquerors imposed burdensome taxes on the peasants who lived throughout the country. For a thousand years, the Vietnamese periodically revolted and tried to remove Chinese rule. But each time, they were unsuccessful.

During the 10th century, the Vietnamese were finally successful in expelling the Chinese conquerors. A leader named Ngo Quyen proved to be more than a match for the Chinese. Although outnumbered by the Chinese forces, Ngo devised a method of defeating them. In 938, he lured the Chinese into a battle along the Bach Dang River. Unknown to the enemy, Ngo Quyen ordered metal spikes sunk into the riverbed at low tide. When the waters rose, the spikes were hidden. Ngo drew the Chinese ships across the hidden spikes, then at low tide he began to lure them backward. The enemy ships were pierced by the spikes and defeated. As a result of this battle, Chinese rule was ended. Over most of the next 1,000 years, the Vietnamese would remain independent.

The Chinese, however, continued to harass Vietnam

Vietnamese Patriots

During the early history of Vietnam, several courageous patriots led their people in revolts against the Chinese. In the first century A.D. a woman named Trung Trac led a band of Vietnamese aristocrats in a revolution after the Chinese had murdered her husband. Joined by her sister, Trung Nhi, they briefly established a Vietnamese kingdom. However, the Trung sisters were eventually overwhelmed by the superior Chinese army. But, instead of surrendering, they jumped into a river and drowned. During the third century, a Vietnamese woman named Trieu Au rode an elephant at the head of her soldiers as she led them into battle against the Chinese conquerors. "I want to . . . sweep the whole country to save people from slavery. . . ." she said. However, she also failed to throw out the Chinese and eventually committed suicide. Another revolt broke out in 543 A.D., led by an aristocrat named Ly Bon. At first Ly Bon carried on a successful guerrilla war against the Chinese, and even became emperor of Vietnam in 544. But two years later, the Chinese defeated him. Ly Bon was captured and beheaded.

and attempted to reconquer it. In the 13th century, the Chinese emperor Kublai Khan sent his navy against the Vietnamese. But the Chinese were again defeated at the Bach Dang River because they fell into the same trap that Ngo Quyen had set for them. During the 15th century, the Chinese were more successful and briefly reasserted control of Vietnam. Once again a patriot appeared, named Le Loi, who led a successful guerrilla campaign against the Chinese. At a decisive battle fought in the Red River Delta in 1426, Le Loi used elephants to terrify the Chinese cavalry and finally defeated them.

Over the next 400 years, Vietnam would be ruled by a series of local kings. But the country was often plagued by unrest and civil war. The kings generally tried to enrich their own followers. In the countryside, wealthy landowners controlled large estates, while the peasants were forced to eke out a meager existence. Nevertheless, they were still heavily taxed by the central government, which relied on this revenue to support the lavish lifestyle of the king. Meanwhile, the Vietnamese rulers began to encounter Western traders. During the 17th century, the Portuguese arrived and helped one powerful Vietnamese royal family in a civil war against another family. In the 17th century, Dutch traders also appeared, followed by the French. In addition to traders, Catholic missionaries came to Vietnam. One of these missionaries was Father Alexandre de Rhodes who baptized thousands of Vietnamese and established a Catholic community in the country. But the Vietnamese emperors regarded the foreign missionaries as a threat to their rule and executed many of them.

Although France's efforts to gain a foothold in Vietnam were temporarily halted, the French did not give up. During the 18th century, a civil war broke out in Vietnam once again. The French helped one side decisively defeat the other and establish a single unified kingdom in Vietnam in 1802. France also continued sending missionaries to Vietnam, although some of them were executed. In 1857, following the execution of a missionary, French Emperor Louis-Napoléon decided to invade Vietnam. In addition to protecting the missionaries, Louis-Napoléon hoped to establish a French colonial empire in Vietnam. By 1859, the French had taken Saigon and began to expand their control throughout the Mekong River Delta. Gradually, French power grew northward until by 1873 Hanoi had also fallen.

The French conquest of Vietnam was part of 19th century imperialism. European nations, including Great Britain, Belgium, and Germany, established large colonial empires in Africa and Asia. A primary purpose of these empires was to exploit the raw materials of the conquered territories. In Vietnam, for example, France exploited the large rice growing areas of the Mekong and Red River Deltas. French planters were given huge plantations, which they operated by using the labor of native Vietnamese peasants. The peasants lost their independence as their land was taken over by the French. In addition, the French brought rubber trees to Vietnam. Large rubber plantations were established, which were owned by wealthy planters and worked by Vietnamese peasants. The French governed the country with a small bureaucracy. They were assisted by native Vietnamese bureaucrats and well-to-do landowners who were happy to cooperate with the French. In return, the French allowed them to retain their lands and share in the revenues collected from the peasants. Meanwhile, the French did not create any industries in Vietnam. They wanted the country to be a market for French manufacturers back in Europe. Any local industries would only provide cheap competition.

During the 1880s, some Vietnamese resorted to a familiar strategy to deal with foreign invaders. They carried on a guerrilla war. The guerrillas established their bases in the mountains of Vietnam. During the night, they would infiltrate villages and disrupt French control. The guerrillas would also try to recruit soldiers among the peasants who were dissatisfied with French rule. But the French proved too powerful for the guerrillas. Using a combination of superior weapons and support among local Vietnamese who had profited from French rule, France finally defeated the guerrilla movement during the 1890s.

This peace was short-lived. In 1907 there was a new revolt that was organized by a resistance leader named Phan Boi Chau. He successfully carried out a plot in which French army officers were poisoned by Vietnamese soldiers who served under them. However, the leaders of the revolt were discovered, and Phan was forced to flee the country. Shortly afterward, another revolt was led by a mandarin named Phan Chu Trinh. But he was captured by the French and imprisoned. Later Phan Chu Trinh was pardoned and allowed to emigrate to France. There he continued to speak out against the French. Phan collected a small group of supporters who included a young man named Nguyen That Thanh.

Thanh had attended college in Vietnam and planned to become a government bureaucrat. But after becoming dissatisfied with French rule, he left Vietnam and went to Paris. Thanh supported himself there by working as a photograph refinisher. Soon he had become a leader of the Vietnamese resistance and changed his name to Nguyen Ai Quoc (the patriot.) At the Paris Peace Conference of 1919, which ended World War I, Nguyen delivered a petition asking the European powers to grant Vietnam its freedom. The petition was immediately rejected. But Nguyen did not give up his efforts to free Vietnam from French rule.

During the 1920s, Nguyen joined the French Communist Party. He traveled to Moscow where he studied at the Lenin School of Oriental Peoples. Eventually, Nguyen returned to Asia, where he began to build local Communist organizations. In 1930, he became the leader of the Vietnamese Communist party. Nguyen had become convinced that only Communist principles could offer the Vietnamese a successful alternative to French rule. During the 1930s, Nguyen led revolts against French rule. He received the support of many peasants whose economic misery had grown even worse because of the worldwide economic depression. The Communists offered the peasants land, which would be taken from the wealthy plantation owners, as well as an end to taxes. At first, the Communist-led revolts were successful. But the French retaliated with enormous military power and rapidly crushed the Communists. Nguyen Ai Quoc was arrested along with his supporters, including Vo Nguyen Giap. There were rumors that Nguyen Ai Quoc had been killed, but he had actually escaped from prison and returned to Moscow.

During the 1930s, the French continued to rule Vietnam. But by 1939, the situation was changing. World War II had begun, and in the following spring, the Nazis conquered France. The Communists still remaining in Vietnam seized the opportunity to revolt. But the French were too powerful for them and quickly put down the uprising. While the Communists were easy to overcome, French forces were no match for an even more powerful enemy—Japan. The fertile rice-producing areas of Vietnam looked very attractive to the Japanese who wanted the rice to feed their armies. By 1941, Japan had taken control of Vietnam, although the French were allowed to handle the day-to-day governing of the country. Nevertheless, the Japanese would take so much rice from Vietnam that the Vietnamese people suffered a severe famine.

Meanwhile, Nguyen Ai Quoc and Vo Nguyen Giap had returned to Vietnam. They had the support of many Vietnamese peasants as well as large segments of the middle class that detested Japanese rule. In 1941, Nguyen Ai Quoc and other Communist leaders established the Vietminh (the Vietnam Independence League). The Vietminh began to organize a guerrilla campaign against the French and the Japanese. At first China was fearful of the growing strength of the Vietminh. The Chinese Nationalists led by President Chiang Kai-shek were already battling against Chinese Communists led by Mao

Nguyen Ai Quoc changed his name to Ho Chi Minh around the time this photograph was taken in the 1940s. He was involved in the efforts to free Vietnam from French and Japanese rule.

Tse-tung for control of China. Chiang Kai-shek did not want the Communists to take control of Vietnam, nor did some Vietnamese political leaders who mistrusted the Communists. Nguyen was arrested and taken to China. Eventually, he was allowed to leave prison after agreeing to lead his guerrilla forces against the Japanese.

By this time, Nguyen had changed his name to Ho Chi Minh to escape attention by the French and Japanese government of Vietnam. From 1943 until 1945, Ho Chi Minh led the Vietminh against the Japanese. The Vietminh received help from American Special Forces and U.S. bombing raids. In 1945, Japan finally ended the French government in Vietnam. The Japanese declared that they would govern the country. But the government lasted only a few months. Following the dropping of atomic bombs on Hiroshima and Nagasaki, Japan surrendered, ending World War II.

At this point, the Vietminh found itself as the only major force in Vietnam. On September 2, 1945, Ho Chi Minh declared that Vietnam was independent. As he put it to a large crowd gathered in Hanoi: "Vietnam has the right to be a free and independent country—and in fact is so already." But France and the United States had no intention of allowing Ho Chi Minh to establish an independent Communist state in Vietnam. And the Vietminh were not powerful enough to oppose the military power of the United States. With American support, French troops returned to Vietnam to reassert control of the country. However, the Vietminh was growing. Ho Chi Minh and his military commander, General Vo Nguyen Giap, vowed that the French would eventually be driven from the country, and they began a guerrilla campaign to achieve their goals.

As the Communists gained support among the peasants in the countryside, the French rapidly found that they were only able to control the urban centers, such as Hanoi. Nevertheless, French leaders were convinced that with U.S. support they could hold the colony. In 1954 the French army had fortified a position in northern Vietnam at Dien Bien Phu. The French base was located in a valley, and they hoped to lure the Vietminh into the area, then defeat the enemy with superior weapons. The French were convinced that Giap and the Vietminh had no artillery that they could bring to the rugged hills that surrounded Dien Bien Phu. But Giap fooled them and laid siege to the French position. Superior Communist forces overran French positions and eventually shut down the airfield. The French had planned to use the airfield to keep their army supplied through airlifts. Meanwhile the steady rains of the monsoon turned the French position at Dien Bien Phu into a quagmire. Finally, on May 7, 1954, the French surrendered to General Giap's forces. It was a victory as important as the battle at Bach Dang in 938 A.D.

Ho Chi Minh confidently expected that the Western powers would now leave Vietnam. But the United States was not ready to allow the entire country to fall into the Communist orbit. Soviet forces had already established Communist satellite governments in eastern Europe. In China, the Communist forces of Mao Tse-tung had taken control of the country and ousted the Chinese nationalists. American foreign policy experts believed in the domino theory. "Communists must be strictly contained," they wrote. "In a shrinking world, the fate of each country is linked to that of all others. The free world is only as strong as its weakest link; thus the fall to communism of any country threatens the security of the United States and so the fate of the entire world itself."

At the Geneva Conference of 1954, Vietnam was divided into northern and southern sections along the 17th parallel. Ho Chi Minh ruled the north. In the south, the United States backed a regime led by a Vietnamese Catholic named Ngo Dinh Diem. Unfortunately, Diem's policies were not much different than those imposed by

French and Vietnamese prisoners marched from the battlefields at Dien Bien Phu after being defeated by the Communist Vietminh army.

the French. As a result, he was successful in controlling the cities in South Vietnam. But in the countryside, he received little support from the peasants. Nevertheless, he continued to receive financial aid from the United States because he hated the Communists and refused to deal with Ho Chi Minh.

Ngo Dinh Diem was the leader of South Vietnam after the country was divided into north and south at the Geneva Conference of 1954.

However, Diem's army in South Vietnam was unsuccessful in dealing with a growing Communist guerrilla force of Vietminh fighters that were still living in the south. Diem called this army the Vietcong. The Vietcong was being supplied from North Vietnam along a series of jungle roads that ran through Laos and Cambodia, known as the Ho Chi Minh Trail.

Diem realized that he was losing the battle against the

Communists, and by 1963 he seemed willing to negotiate with Ho Chi Minh. However, the United States did not want to negotiate. As a result, the United States permitted the South Vietnamese military to stage a coup against Diem that resulted in his death. By this time, the United States had committed over 16,000 military advisers to the war. In addition, the United States was conducting bombing raids on South Vietnamese villages designed to root out the Vietcong. Nevertheless, no end to the war was in sight. When President John F. Kennedy was assassinated late in 1963, the policy of the United States in South Vietnam was simply to assist the Vietnamese government in its battle to defeat the Communists.

Flames from a Vietcong rocket attack on an American base light up the sky in Da Nang.

The Beginning of Tet

In December 1963, President Lyndon Johnson sent his secretary of defense, Robert McNamara to South Vietnam. McNamara's job was to evaluate the situation, that is, to determine how the war was going and return with a full report for the president. What McNamara eventually told Johnson was discouraging. He believed that unless the current situation was changed soon, it could easily lead to "neutralization at best or more likely to a Communist-controlled state." In other words, South Vietnam and its ally, the United States, were losing the battle against the Communists.

Coincidentally, the political leaders in North Vietnam were conducting an assessment of the war at almost exactly the same time. What they saw troubled them, too. Although the Vietcong had been trying to undermine the government of South Vietnam for almost 10 years, victory was no closer. The United States seemed to have no intention of withdrawing from Southeast Asia. Indeed, the war had reached a stalemate. The only alternative was for North Vietnam to send its own troops into the south to strengthen the forces of the Vietcong. As the Communist leaders put it: "The key point at present is to make outstanding efforts to strengthen rapidly our military forces in order to create a basic change in the balance of forces between the enemy and ourselves in South Vietnam."

To enable North Vietnam to move more men and material into the south, its political leaders decided to improve the Ho Chi Minh Trail. In 1964, Colonel Dong Si Nguyen, began to transform the series of jungle trails into a modern supply route. His engineers constructed roads and bridges, created gun positions to protect the route against American bombing raids, built hospitals to treat the wounded, and constructed supply depots to feed troops heading into South Vietnam. During 1964, an estimated 10,000 North Vietnamese traveled southward with improved weapons. These included mortars and rocket launchers supplied by China and the Soviet Union. By the end of the year, the Vietcong were conducting more powerful raids. In December, they took over the village of Binh Gia, located only 40 miles southeast of Saigon. When South Vietnamese troops came to dislodge the Communists, they disappeared into the jungle—but only briefly. When the South Vietnamese pursued them, the Vietcong ambushed their pursuers, killing 200 of them as well as 5 American advisers.

Meanwhile, the United States had been moving slowly to increase its commitment to South Vietnam. In 1964, President Johnson had appointed a new American commander in Vietnam, General William C. Westmoreland.

General William C. Westmoreland addresses infantrymen after he was appointed commander in Vietnam in 1964.

The president had also ordered secret raids against North Vietnam. In addition, American ships entered the Gulf of Tonkin off the coast of North Vietnam to monitor Communist military operations. In August 1964 one of these ships—the destroyer *Maddox*—engaged in a brief battle with North Vietnam torpedo boats. Johnson retaliated with bombing missions against North Vietnam. In addition, he asked the Congress to pass the Gulf of Tonkin Resolution. On August 7, by an overwhelming vote, the president was given power to take "all necessary measures" to repel attacks against U.S. forces and "to prevent further aggression."

At this point, President Johnson hesitated to take any further steps. He was in the midst of a presidential election campaign and did not want the voters to believe that he was leading America into war. Therefore, Johnson waited until after the election and his resounding victory before making any other military moves.

In the early morning hours of February 7, 1965, Vietcong attacked the South Vietnamese military base of Pleiku. Located in the central part of the country, Pleiku was a starting point for South Vietnamese raids against the Ho Chi Minh Trail. The Vietcong attack left 8 American advisers dead and approximately 100 wounded. Several weeks later, General Westmoreland received the first American marines sent to South Vietnam. Their job was to protect the airfield at Da Nang, along the northern coast of Vietnam, which was also threatened by Vietcong.

Vietcong attacks continued during 1965. The Communists hit a provincial capital only 50 miles north of Saigon, as well as a nearby camp where American Special Forces were stationed. The government of Vietnam was clearly incapable of stopping the Vietcong attacks. In June, new military officers took control of the government. General Nguyen Van Thieu became president, and Air Vice Marshal Nguyen Cao Ky became prime minister.

In the meantime, the number of American troops was gradually increasing. Indeed, President Johnson had already become convinced that hundreds of thousands of soldiers might be necessary to stop the Vietcong and their North Vietnamese allies. In addition, the Americans under-took massive military building projects in South Vietnam to provide airfields and naval bases for their military build up. These included an expansion of the airbase at Da Nang and new harbors along the South Vietnamese coast, such as the base at Camranh Bay. By 1967, over 400,000 American troops were already committed to the fighting in South Vietnam. Meanwhile, North Vietnam was sending 20,000 soldiers a month along the Ho Chi Minh Trail into the south. The United States hoped that the continued

North Vietnamese photographer Trong Thanh spent five years documenting traffic on the Ho Chi Minh Trail. The people of North Vietnam carried food and ammunition along the trail.

bombing of the north and the Ho Chi Minh Trail, known as Operation Rolling Thunder, might eventually persuade the Communists to call off the war. But the bombing seemed to be having little effect. As historian Stanley Karnow wrote, the Vietcong needed few supplies to maintain their war effort. Unlike the Americans, the Vietcong did not rely on tanks or airplanes to carry on the war. What food or ammunition they needed could be transported along the Ho Chi Minh Trail regardless of the bombing. Meanwhile, in the north, there were always thousands of people ready to be recruited by the government to repair any damage done by American bombers to roads, bridges, or railroads.

In South Vietnam, American troops worked with the Army of the Republic of (South) Vietnam (ARVN) to safeguard the countryside and push out the Vietcong. In early 1967, for example, Americans and ARVN forces attacked an area known as the Iron Triangle north of Saigon. The attack was devastating. Heavy bombing destroyed major villages in the area and burned out farms in an effort to eliminate any Vietcong hiding places. Initially, the allied attack was successful and the Vietcong were driven away with heavy losses. But several months later they began returning to the Iron Triangle, and by the end of the year they had established a new base of operations there.

The American experience in the Iron Triangle epitomized the frustration of fighting in South Vietnam. No matter how powerful the weapons or how much devastation was caused, it was not enough to stop the Vietcong. The Vietnamese were successfully resorting to the same type of guerrilla warfare they had used for centuries to defeat their enemies. In the meantime, the campaigns of the Americans and the ARVN were alienating the peasants in the countryside. Thousands had already fled from their villages, leaving them to the Vietcong. The displaced peasants went to South Vietnamese cities such as Saigon. However, there were often no jobs and little food for them there. Neither the South Vietnamese government nor the Americans could give the peasants what they needed.

General Vo Nguyen Giap is shown here visiting his troops in North Vietnam. He designed a far-reaching battle plan that was supposed to defeat the American and South Vietnamese forces.

By the end of 1967, the war in Vietnam had again reached a stalemate. The Americans and North Vietnamese had vastly increased their commitment to the battlefield. But neither side could defeat the enemy. In the North, General Giap had already decided on a bold new strategy aimed at eventually breaking the deadlock. It involved a series of simultaneous attacks against American bases and South Vietnamese cities. Giap targeted cities such as Saigon in the south, Nha Trang and Qui Nhon in central South Vietnam, as well as Quang Ngai and Hue in the northern part of the country. His aim was to undermine the confidence of the South Vietnamese civilians living in the cities as well as the peasants who had fled there from the countryside. Giap hoped to prove to them that there was no safety anywhere in South Vietnam. Neither the government nor American power could protect average citizens from the Vietcong. As a result, Giap hoped, the South Vietnamese would lose all confidence in their government, which would eventually be toppled by the Communists. In addition, Americans, who had been repeatedly told by the Johnson Administration that their troops were winning the war, would be shaken in their support of the war effort. The peace protests in America would grow. Pressure would, therefore, build on the U.S. government to rethink the war and begin to disengage from South Vietnam.

While Giap's major targets were the South Vietnamese cities, he hoped to confuse the American high command by attacking some of their principal military bases. These included Khe Sanh along the Laotian border, and Pleiku further south. American Special Forces had originally set up Khe Sanh in 1962. It was among a series of bases established near the demilitarized zone separating North and South Vietnam. These bases stretched from the border with Laos to the city of Hue in the east. By attacking Khe Sanh, Giap hoped to convince General Westmoreland to concentrate his troops there, while the Vietcong infiltrated the cities.

During the fall of 1967, the North Vietnamese began to attack allied positions in the northern part of South Vietnam, along the Cambodian border. General Westmoreland retaliated with massive bombing raids that staggered the enemy and produced an enormous number of casualties. Westmoreland had also received reports that the North Vietnamese were massing to attack the base at Khe Sanh. For several years, Westmoreland had hoped to engage the North Vietnamese in a traditional battle instead of the usual hit-and-run guerrilla campaign. The American general was convinced that in such a confrontation, the United States could destroy the enemy and perhaps win a decisive battle that might turn the tide of the war. Already, American commanders believed that the war was moving in their favor. They seemed to be inflicting heavier casualties on the Vietcong. And it seemed impossible that superior American technology could not eventually win a victory in Vietnam. As a result, Westmoreland and his advisers were not prepared for simultaneous attacks against American bases and South Vietnamese cities. They did not believe that the Vietcong and the North Vietnamese had such a powerful military capability.

This was exactly what General Giap and Ho Chi Minh had wanted. On January 1, 1968, Radio Hanoi broadcast a poem written by Ho. It read:

> This Spring far outshines the
>   previous Springs,
>
> Of triumphs throughout the land
>   come happy tidings.
>
> Let North and South emulate each
>   other in fighting the U.S. aggressors!
>
> Forward!
>
> Total Victory will be ours.

This was the signal that an attack was about to begin. Already, Vietcong had infiltrated the major cities, carrying weapons that they could use during the offensive. And vast shipments of supplies for Communist troops were moving down the Ho Chi Minh Trail. But the Vietcong had not been able to conceal all of their maneuvers from the Americans. Intercepted enemy orders told of an attack on

The Antagonists: General Westmoreland and General Giap

William Childs Westmoreland was born in Spartanburg, South Carolina, in 1914. As a child, he became an Eagle Scout. Later he attended West Point Military Academy where he graduated in 1936. There he was called "Westy," a nickname that would always remain with him. As a cadet, he was given the John J. Pershing award for being an outstanding leader. Westmoreland commanded an artillery battalion during World War II, serving in North Africa and Sicily. He was almost killed when his truck ran over a land mine. Westmoreland also served in the Korean War in 1952 where he gained a reputation as a fearless paratroops commander. He worked the men in his battalion very hard, saying, "By 10 o'clock every night, they were so exhausted they couldn't make mischief of any kind." Westmoreland returned to West Point in 1960, as commandant of the facility. By that time he had already become the youngest major general in the army. Four years later, he went to Vietnam, becoming commander in chief in 1964. In 1965, *Time* magazine named Westmoreland their Man of the Year. As *Time* put it: "A jut-jawed six-footer, he never smokes, drinks little, swims and plays tennis to remain . . . only 10 lbs. over his cadet weight. . . . Westmoreland belongs to the age of technology—a product not only of combat but also of sophisticated command and management colleges."

■   ■   ■

Commanding the North Vietnamese was Vo Nguyen Giap, whose background was entirely different. Born in 1911 in the village of An Xa, Giap, left home at the age of 12 to attend a French school in Hue. According to his own account, the French later expelled him from the school because he was involved in revolutionary activities. During the 1930s, Giap joined the Vietnamese Communist Party, where he worked with Ho Chi Minh in China. As the war with Japan began, Giap and Ho led the Vietminh against the Japanese army and the French bureaucrats that ran the Vietnamese government. During World War II and afterward, Giap honed his skills as a guerrilla leader. One of his idols was a 13th century guerrilla leader named Tran Hung Dao whose guerrilla tactics defeated a huge army of Mongols that were trying to take control of Vietnam. Giap also learned guerrilla warfare from Mao Tse-tung. His most famous victory occurred in 1954 against the French at Dien Bien Phu. During the Vietnam War, he took command of the Peoples' Army of North Vietnam (PAVN) and directed the war against South Vietnam and the United States.

Pleiku and Ban Me Thuot. Near the end of January, Vietcong soldiers inside Saigon had been arrested with tapes that were to be broadcast during an uprising against the government. But the American high command refused to believe that the Communists could strike so many areas at once.

Westmoreland was still convinced that the battle would be waged at Khe Sanh. He also thought it would begin sometime before or just after the lunar new year, which was known as Tet. This was a holiday throughout North and South Vietnam when families gathered together for celebrations. The Americans did not believe that the Communists would stage an offensive during the holiday. Therefore, the American high command did not pay attention when in the north the day of the holiday was changed from January 30 to one day earlier. This would give North Vietnamese time to celebrate before the battle. Nor were the Americans aware that during the late 18th century, the Vietnamese had launched an attack during Tet against the Chinese that were occupying Hanoi.

General Westmoreland focused his attentions on Khe Sanh as well as Hue. He was convinced that the North Vietnamese attacks would stay as close as possible to their own country to reduce the need for long supply lines. He also reasoned that General Giap might try to capture the northern part of South Vietnam and incorporate it into his own country. Westmoreland was ready. Code-named Operation Niagara, his plan called for surveillance to pinpoint North Vietnamese positions, then a massive bombing raid to destroy them. In addition, he had strengthened the military forces at Khe Sanh to defend against the enemy attack. On January 21, 1968, the army of North Vietnam began to attack the marines at Khe Sanh. The battle had begun.

Attack on Saigon

Soldiers from South Vietnam had to protect their capital city of Saigon (now called Ho Chi Minh City) from a massive Communist attack. The attack came at a time when many in the military were with their families celebrating Tet, the festival of the lunar new year.

During the war, Saigon, the capital of South Vietnam, had escaped any devastation. A large contingent of ARVN soldiers and government police patrolled the city. Saigon was also protected by the large American air base at Tan Son Nhut and other U.S. military installations in the area. Indeed, Saigon had become a safe haven for Vietnamese peasants fleeing the war in the country-side. As more and more peasants came to the city, its population swelled to three million, including the people who lived in the surrounding suburbs. Unfortunately, there was little work for many of the refugees, but at least they had escaped the destructive war that had laid waste to so much of the country.

The Tet Offensive would show all South Vietnamese that no area of their country was safe from the enemy. On January 30, 1968, a force of 100,000 Communist troops began a coordinated attack throughout South Vietnam. They had been ordered to: "Move forward to achieve final victory." They were urged to "display to the utmost your revolutionary heroism by surmounting all hardships and difficulties and making sacrifices as to be able to fight continually and aggressively." Finally, they were assured that Tet was "the greatest battle ever fought throughout the history of our country."

The North Vietnamese and Vietcong had targeted more than three-quarters of the provincial capitals and most of the major cities, including Hue and Da Nang in the north, Bon Me Thuot and Pleiku in the center of the country, as well as Phan Thiet and Saigon in the south. Pleiku, for example, was hit in the early morning hours of January 30. One U.S. Army nurse who was serving at Pleiku said: "The Vietcong seemed to think that the red crosses on our tents were targets at which to aim."

While South Vietnamese cities were being hit throughout the country, Saigon remained quiet—or, at least, relatively so. The people there were in the midst of celebrating the lunar new year, ushering in the Year of the Monkey. They were setting off fireworks throughout the city. But intelligence indicated that Saigon would soon be hit. The Vietcong had already infiltrated the city with about 5,000 of their soldiers dressed as civilians. One of them was captured by the ARVN and told them under interrogation that Tan Son Nhut airbase and Saigon were about to be attacked. However, President Nguyen Van Thieu had permitted half the ARVN troops to take leave so they could celebrate the Tet holiday with their families. As a result, the city was not fully defended.

During the early morning hours of January 31, the attack on Saigon began from several different directions. Led by battle-hardened North Vietnamese general Tran Do, the battle plan called for the Communists to attack key positions in Saigon while also launching an assault on the American bases outside the city. This would prevent U.S. reinforcements from entering Saigon. Among the first targets was the U.S. embassy. The symbol of American power, it was protected by a concrete rocket shield and outside of it was an eight-foot wall. But the embassy was only lightly defended by two American military police (MP) at the gates and a few marines inside. The Vietcong fired a rocket that tore a hole in the wall of the embassy and killed the two American MPs. But before they died, the American defenders had killed the leaders of the Communist assault. Nevertheless, the Communists launched a rocket that penetrated the main building of the embassy and exploded in the lobby. By this time, however, the attack was leaderless and the Vietcong never entered any of the buildings. The marines inside the building held out until they were reinforced by the 101st Airborne Division, which killed all the remaining Vietcong.

Meanwhile, Communist soldiers were also attacking the presidential palace. As they destroyed the gate with rockets, the Vietcong were immediately struck by a hail of gunfire from the defenders. The Vietcong retreated to an apartment building where they tried to hold off attacks by ARVN soldiers and U.S. MPs over the next two days. Eventually all the attackers were killed or captured. The Vietcong had also planned to seize the radio station in Saigon. They had prepared a series of tapes to be broadcast over the radio throughout South Vietnam, announcing that Saigon had fallen and the people should rise up and throw out the government.

A Shocking Scene

On February 2, 1968, Americans sitting in their living rooms witnessed a shocking scene on the evening news. The chief of the South Vietnam National Police, Nguyen Ngoc Loan, stood near a Vietcong officer. The officer was not dressed in a uniform but wore a short-sleeve plaid shirt and short pants. His hands were tied behind his back. Suddenly, Loan took out a revolver, pointed it at the head of the enemy officer, and pulled the trigger. The man fell to the ground and died. This picture emphasized the brutality of the war in Vietnam. Although television cameras had covered the battle that raged around the presidential palace, this scene reduced the bloodshed of war to the death of an individual at the hands of another. Although the Vietcong officer had seemingly been executed for no reason, there was more to the story. Some of Loan's police had been killed by the Vietcong that had also invaded the home of one policemen and murdered his entire family. Loan was extremely upset and took out his anger on a single prisoner. Pictures like this one began to convince many Americans that the United States should not continue participating in the war.

By controlling the radio station, the Vietcong hoped to seize the propaganda initiative and persuade the South Vietnamese people that the war was over.

However, the Vietcong plans were quickly foiled. As 20 Vietcong began their assault, a technician at the station radioed to a transmitting tower several miles away that all communications wires should be cut with Saigon. Without any connection to the tower, radio broadcasts quickly became impossible. Nevertheless, the Vietcong wreaked havoc in the station before ARVN soldiers shot them.

Meanwhile, battles were raging throughout the streets of Saigon. Vietcong briefly took over the South Vietnamese Armored Command Headquarters, hoping to find artillery to use in their attacks. But nothing was there. The Communists were also going from house to

South Vietnamese National Police Chief Brigadier General Nguyen Ngoc Loan is shown executing a Vietcong officer in 1968 in this famous photograph. The officer was dressed in civilian clothes and was carrying a pistol when he was caught and brought to the police chief.

house looking for government bureaucrats or Americans. Once they were discovered, they were rounded up in the street and some of them were shot. The South Vietnamese also killed some Vietcong prisoners without ever putting them on trial.

While the battle continued inside Saigon, the Vietcong also attacked American military installations outside the city. Tan Son Nhut air base—headquarters of U.S. military forces, known as the Military Assistance Command Vietnam (MACV)—bore the brunt of a massive assault. Tan Son Nhut was especially critical to the Vietcong plans because it was not only headquarters of the U.S. command, but South Vietnamese high ranking officials were there, too. The Vietcong hoped to assassinate President Thieu and Vice President Ky. The Communists successfully attacked an ARVN guard post and penetrated within the base. The American command had been caught off guard, not expecting an assault on such an important installation. Most of the senior American soldiers, including senior staff, were not even armed. However, the Communists were met with fire from the ARVN Eighth Airborne Battalion which held them back. American officers also joined in the attack and they eventually received reinforcements from the American 25th Infantry Division coming in from nearby Cu Chi. U.S. tanks forced the Vietcong to retreat to a textile mill on the outskirts of the base. The mill was pounded by American aircraft until the Communist position was finally destroyed.

Within a few days, U.S. and ARVN forces had defeated the Vietcong assaults in the Saigon area. However, fighting continued in some parts of Saigon during February. On February 4, American jets pounded Vietcong positions in the Cholon section of Saigon after asking the residents to evacuate. Cholon was devastated, but the Communists still retained a position at the nearby Phu Tho racetrack. Finally, on February 10th, the American 199th Light Infantry Brigade destroyed the remaining Vietcong defensive posts.

In other parts of South Vietnam, cities were also

The Cholon area of Saigon was destroyed as Americans attacked the
Vietcong defensive post there.

List of Acronyms

ARVN	Army of the Republic of Vietnam
DMZ	demilitarized zone
DRV	Democratic Republic of Vietnam—North Vietnam
JCS	joint chiefs of staff
MACV	Military Assistance Command, Vietnam—U.S. high command
NLF	National Liberation Front
NVA	North Vietnamese Army
I Corps	Eye Corps—Allied command of northern provinces of South Vietnam
RVNAF	Republic of Vietnam Armed Forces
VC	Vietcong

struck by the Vietcong. Da Nang withstood a rocket attack that destroyed American aircraft before the attackers were defeated in house-to-house fighting. Along the coast, Hoi An and Qui Nhon, which had been safe from the war, were also attacked. However, the Communists were unsuccessful in maintaining their positions in the cities for very long. Similar results occurred in Pleiku and Ban Me Thuot, which were eventually cleared of Vietcong soldiers in a few days.

The Vietcong attacks on the cities, including Saigon, had been unsuccessful. As President Johnson put it: "We have known for some time that this offensive was planned by the enemy. The ability to do what they have done has been anticipated, prepared for, and met." The North Vietnamese and Vietcong had tried to hit too many places at once, and many of the attacks were uncoordinated. However, they had shown the U.S. commanders that Communist armies were a powerful force that could strike at will anywhere in South Vietnam.

The attacks on Saigon and other cities was only part of the Tet Offensive. The next phase would be even more ferocious as Communists assaulted Hue and Khe Sanh.

Hue City

Vietcong bombs exploded in the moat surrounding the citadel of Hue City. The Communists were attempting to take control of the city during the Tet Offensive.

The city of Hue was a link between past and present in Vietnam. With its wide avenues, spacious homes, and beautiful walled gardens, Hue had become the imperial capital during the 19th century. Emperor Gia Long had constructed a powerful citadel to defend the city and his magnificent palace. The citadel was protected by a thick brick wall, while farther out was another wall that was 30-feet high, and beyond this wall was a moat connected to the Perfume River. On the other side of the river lay the rest of Hue City. When Vietnam was divided, Hue became the key to the northern provinces of South Vietnam, called I Corps by the American high command. Lying only about

60 miles south of the demilitarized zone, Hue could easily be attacked by the North Vietnamese. But during the early part of the war, Hue had escaped any conflict. However, many of the Buddhists who lived in the city were opposed to the regime in Saigon and sympathetic to the aims of the Vietcong. In fact, Buddhist protests in 1963 had helped bring an end to the Diem government.

As part of the Tet Offensive, the Communists hoped to take control of Hue. In early January, Vietcong troops, disguised as civilians, entered the city to help coordinate the coming attacks. From its intelligence sources, the U.S. high command had received some information indicating that a Communist assault might happen at any time. General Westmoreland had sent this information to Washington, but nothing was done to strengthen the city's defenses. Just before the Tet Offensive began, the American base at nearby Phu Bai picked up Communist radio communications indicating an attack. But the attack had already started before this intelligence reached Hue.

Inside the city, the citadel was defended by the ARVN First Division under the command of General Ngo Quang Truong. Because of the Tet holiday, General Truong's forces were not at full strength, and some of them were outside the citadel on reconnaissance duty. In the early morning hours of January 31, the citadel was attacked by rocket fire as the North Vietnamese advanced under cover of a dense fog. The Communist attack was led by units of the North Vietnamese Fifth and Sixth Regiments. As rockets ripped into the walls of the citadel, Communist troops advanced against Tay Loc airfield inside the fortress. Here they were met by the ARVN Black Panthers who were successful in holding onto the airfield until they were eventually overwhelmed by a Communist onslaught. The North Vietnamese rapidly took control of most of the citadel, pushing

Lieutenant General Ngo Quang Truong was the commander of the First Division of the Army of the Republic of Vietnam. He was in charge of defending the citadel at Hue.

General Truong and his men into defensive positions in one corner.

Across the Perfume River, in the southern part of Hue, Communist forces had also made impressive gains. The communists had rapidly taken over key strategic points, including police stations, a hospital, and government buildings. They had also targeted the U.S. Military Assistance

Command, Vietnam (MACV) center, a walled building that had formerly been a hotel. But here they met stiff resistance from about 300 defenders who stopped the Communist advance. The defenders called for reinforcements from Phu Bai. But initially the American commanders believed that there had been only a small Communist attack on Hue. At Phu Bai, Brigadier General Foster Lahue found himself facing a difficult decision. Charged with defending a large area from Hue to Da Nang, he could not send too many of his troops to one location and leave others undefended. Therefore, he decided to send only a single company—A Company, First Battalion, First Marines—commanded by Captain Gordon Batcheller.

As Batcheller and his men advanced they were met by several U.S. tanks, and together the combined forces headed for Hue. The relief force crossed the Phu Cam Canal south of the city. As they reached the outskirts of Hue, Batcheller's troops came under a withering attack from North Vietnamese units. Although the American tanks and infantry tried to move forward, they were not strong enough to overcome the Communists that had taken up strong defensive positions among the city's buildings. Batcheller called for reinforcements and another marine company was sent up from Phu Bai. In the mean time, Batcheller was severely wounded in the thigh and the knee by North Vietnamese Army (NVA) machine gunners. Eventually, reinforcements arrived and succeeded in pushing their way into the southern part of the city and reaching the defenders at MACV headquarters. Although this position was now secure, the Communists had taken control of the rest of the southern half of Hue as well as most of the citadel, including the Imperial Palace. Meanwhile, other Communist units had cut off Highway 1, leading out of the city, which served

U.S. Army Infantry Units

Squad	Ten enlisted men commanded by a sergeant
Platoon	Four squads commanded by a lieutenant
Company	Three platoons commanded by a captain
Battalion	Three to five companies commanded by a lieutenant colonel, 600-1,000 troops
Brigade	Three plus battalions and headquarters commanded by a colonel, 3,000 troops
Division	Three brigades, artillery, headquarters, and support units commanded by a major general, 12,000-18,000 troops
Corps	Two plus divisions and support units, commanded by a lieutenant general
Army	Two plus corps under a general

as a potential route for American reinforcements.

In southern Hue, the Communists instituted a new political regime over the city. Revolutionary Committees were put in charge of neighborhood blocks and told to convert the citizens to Communism. They held indoctrination meetings and ordered residents of Hue out of their homes and into the streets to attend the meetings. The Communists were especially interested in any Americans or government officials that might be hiding in their houses. These men were immediately ordered to appear. But many feared for their lives and stayed inside or tried to leave the city. The Communists pursued them doggedly, going from house to house until many of these men were found. "Captured in the home of Vietnamese friends, Stephen Miller of the U.S. Information Service was shot in a field behind a Catholic seminary. Dr. Horst Gunther Krainick, a German physician teaching at the

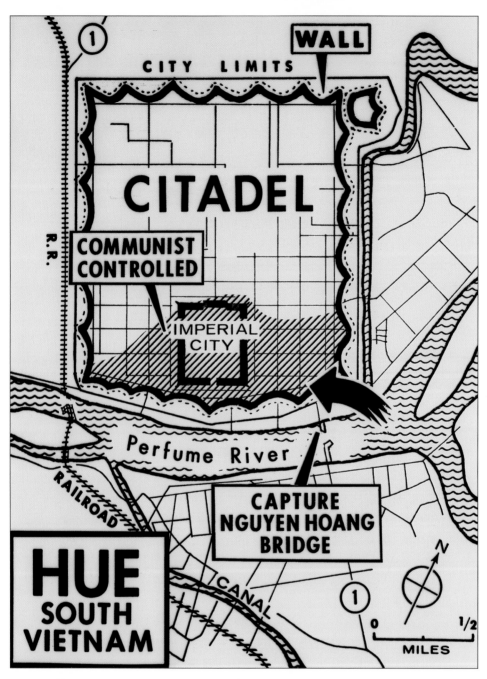

Intense fighting took place between the North Vietnamese troops and the combined U.S.-South Vietnam army. This map illustrates the forces at the citadel and the site where the U.S. Marines captured the Nguyen Hoang Bridge.

local medical school, was seized with his wife and two other German doctors, and their bodies were found in a shallow pit. . . . [Communists] also killed father Buu Dong, a popular Vietnamese Catholic priest who had entertained Vietcong agents in his rectory." In total, an estimated 3,000 civilians were murdered by the Communists while they controlled the city.

While the Communists were trying to maintain their hold on Hue, American and South Vietnamese troops were mounting a counterattack. In the citadel, General Truong had already been reinforced by ARVN units that had cut their way through the North Vietnamese defenders. Truong's troops gradually began to push back the North Vietnamese, although they had been heavily reinforced and told to hold their positions.

In the southern part of the city, the American troops had also been bolstered by additional units from Phu Bai. Although the Americans tried to assault the citadel, they were driven back by the Communists. However, during the first week of February, U.S. forces began a difficult house-to-house fight against the enemy to take control of the southern part of Hue. It was a vicious fight, as the North Vietnamese battled fiercely for every inch of territory. The Communists had also been reinforced by battalions that had come in from west of the city. In addition, the monsoon rains made U.S. attacks by helicopters or jets far more difficult. U.S. Marines used every weapon available to them—tear gas, grenades, artillery, and tanks. Gradually, they began to retake one position after another. The treasury building, the Hue hospital, and the provincial headquarters fell to the American forces. As one battalion commander put it: "Probably the greatest attribute [of the marines] is the fact that people, regardless of their rank, performed at levels that you would seldom see."

More reinforcements marched toward Hue to

strengthen the U.S. attack. Among these troops were units of the 101st Airborne Division. One inexperienced lieutenant, leading a platoon, recalled his first major encounter with the Vietcong. "We came past the paddies," he said, "the trees, came around the green. I looked up and saw an NVA flag flying over the next open space. I couldn't believe it. . . . All I knew at that point was 'My God! I'm scared. . . . This is the real thing." The lieutenant led his men through a bamboo thicket, and they took up a defensive position behind a large mound of dirt. "I got up and I ran around yelling 'Move this machine gun over here' and 'Do this over there'. " All the time, the lieutenant seemed oblivious to the *ping, ping, ping* of enemy bullets whizzing around his head. He had somehow overcome his fear and just did what he had been trained to do. Although the enemy fire was fierce, the lieutenant and his platoon eventually cleared the area and continued to advance toward Hue. "I don't know how I survived that day," he said later. Some of his men, however, were not so lucky.

What had brought the 101st Airborne advancing to Hue was another battle going on northwest of the city for control of supply routes. Americans were airlifted into the area and took control of a hill. From this position, they began to bombard Communist forces in a nearby valley. A counterattack by the North Vietnamese troops, however, forced the Americans to abandon their hill position. Finally, after a fierce battle in the village of Thong Bon Tri, the American troops drove the North Vietnamese from the area.

By February 10 the American forces had finally taken back control of the south side of Hue. The North Vietnamese commander had wanted to evacuate this area several days earlier, but he was told to hold on as long as possible. Even after February 10, however, Communists continued to fire mortar rounds from the north side of the Perfume River against the allied positions in the south.

Inside the citadel, ARVN forces had been under constant attack. General Truong had been defending his position against NVA troops that were constantly being strengthened by reinforcements. Although ARVN soldiers had tried to counterattack, the Communists continued to hold their positions and the ARVN was losing momentum. The difficult job of recapturing the citadel would now fall to the marines. On February 13 they began their assault. The strength of the Communist position in the citadel made it clear that heavy bombing would be necessary to dislodge them. During the first two days of the attack, however, the weather was stormy and aircraft missions were impossible. The marines and the ARVN faced a deadly struggle with the North Vietnamese troops that were dug into strong defensive positions throughout the citadel. As marine officer Myron Harrington put it when he entered the northern part of Hue: "My first impression was of desolation, utter devastation. There were burnt-out tanks and trucks, and upturned automobiles still smoldering. Bodies lay every-where, most of them civilians. The smoke and stench blended, like in some kind of horror movie—except that it lacked weird music. You felt that something could happen at any minute, that they would jump out and start shooting from every side."

The North Vietnamese and Vietcong did start shoot-ing. And the marines were hit with heavy casualties. "As a marine, I had to admire the courage and discipline of the North Vietnamese and the Vietcong, but no more than I did my own men," Harrington recalled. "We were both in a face-to-face, eyeball-to-eyeball confrontation. Sometimes they were only twenty or thirty yards from us, and once we killed a sniper only ten yards away. After a while, survival was the name of the game as you sat there in the semidarkness, with the firing going on constantly, like at a rifle range. And the horrible smell. You tasted it as you ate your rations, as if you were eating death."

The marines hit the Communist forces with heavy artillery. And they also called in repeated air strikes. The enemy was struck by helicopter gun ships, American bombers, and napalm. However, 60 U.S. helicopters were hit, as well as some navy boats along the Perfume River, bringing in supplies to the marines. The intense fighting continued for more than a week. On February 16 the Americans intercepted an enemy communication indicating that the North Vietnamese commander in the citadel had been killed. His replacement was ready to retreat, but the top North Vietnamese command ordered him to hold his position. Meanwhile the bombing intensified. An estimated 50 percent of the city was damaged or destroyed. And 116,000 citizens became homeless, approximately 80 percent of the population.

West of the city, the U.S. First Air Cavalry had cut off the supply routes, so the Communists were almost completely trapped inside the citadel. By February 22, the United States and ARVN had recaptured almost every position except the Imperial Palace. But the NVA/VC were not done fighting. They mounted a counterattack, allowing some of their commanders to escape from the city. By February 24, however, most of the enemy strength had been spent. At 5:00 A.M., the Communist flag on the Imperial Palace was taken down and the flag of South Vietnam was put in its place by the ARVN Black Panthers.

According to one source, "Some correspondents traveling with the soldiers called the fighting in Hue the most intense in South Vietnam. Soldiers had little sleep, and the casualty rate was approximated at one casualty per yard of

This view from the Hue citadel in 1968 shows the once-beautiful ancient city in ruins.

ground gained." Communist losses in the battle were estimated at over 5,000 killed. American troops suffered over 200 killed and almost 1,400 seriously wounded. ARVN forces lost almost 400 dead and almost 2,000 wounded. According to historian Wilbur Morrison: "In large part the allied victory at Hue was due to the men of South Vietnam's 1st Division who held on to their headquarters in the [citadel] and from there continued to direct operations from outside. . . . The South Vietnamese troops, although few in number, had demonstrated high morale and fought superbly despite repeated calls from the communists to surrender." However, the U.S. Marine forces also played a critical role, clearing the Communists out of the southern part of Hue and launching successful attacks against the Communists in the citadel. As one marine commander put it: "I'll never forget how courageous those youngsters were. . . . Everyone was frightened stiff; however, I saw no evidence of cowardice or Marines breaking under stress. . . . Everyone did the best they could, while some performed with extraordinary courage." Indeed, the U.S. First Marines received a special commendation from President Johnson for defeating a large force of the enemy and demonstrating "heroism and daring," during the Hue campaign.

Both sides believed they had won a victory at Hue. The Communists had demonstrated they could occupy an important city, thought to be safe from war and under the control of the allies. On the other hand, the U.S. and ARVN forces had eventually driven the NVA/Vietcong out of Hue and regained control of the city for the government of South Vietnam. Nevertheless, it had been an extremely hard fought battle. And in its opening stages, the American high command had been completely surprised by the audacity of the North Vietnamese and Vietcong attacks. American intelligence had failed to pick up the danger signs of an impending Communist assault until it was too late. North Vietnamese units that fought in the Hue battle were not supposed to have been in the area. In short, it was a failure of U.S. military preparedness, although the final outcome was a victory on the battlefield.

The cost to the people of Hue, however, was catastrophic. Their homes and livelihoods had been destroyed.

Almost 6,000 of them had been killed, and a once beautiful city had been devastated. For a short time, they had also been under control of a Communist government that had wantonly executed innocent citizens. In mid-February, the NVA had tried to retain its hold on Hue by shifting reinforcements to the city from the battle around Khe Sanh. But by then, it was too late. Hue had been lost, and the NVA was also losing the struggle for Khe Sanh.

Khe Sanh

An overview of Khe Sanh shows the U.S. military base at Khe Sanh on South Vietnam's northern border.

ocated near the demilitarized zone, Khe Sanh was a key element in the defense of I Corps in South Vietnam. The village of Khe Sanh lay along Route 9, which crossed South Vietnam from the border with Laos and served as a major supply route. Much of Route 9, however, was extremely narrow and trucks had to move slowly along it to carry supplies to military installations. Khe Sanh was near an old military base called the French Fort, which was occupied by American Special Forces, the Green Berets, in the fall of 1962. North of the fort, an airstrip was carved out from a piece of level ground among the hills to supply troops in the region. American soldiers who came there in 1962 were struck by the isolation of Khe Sanh, miles away from any major city. They also remembered the size of the rats that infested the old French Fort. "One time we went into the village," an American soldier said, "and bought some metal rat traps because it was so bad. We were using mosquito nets on our bunks to keep the rats off. I remember one night there was a big metal rat trap with teeth on it. And I remember the first rat we got. When [the trap] snapped it woke me up. And then the rat started dragging the thing off!"

In the early days of the war, Khe Sanh served as an outpost for American military forces to spy on activity along the Ho Chi Minh Trail, which ran through nearby Laos. Khe Sanh also acted as a trip wire. In case of a full-scale invasion from the north, Khe Sanh would be hit first and warn of the NVA attack on South Vietnam. During 1964 the Special Forces built a new base next to the airstrip so it would be easier to defend. They created strong cement bunkers for the command center and defensive positions. Supplying the base, however, was not easy because of the weather. Especially during the monsoon season, heavy rain storms and low visibility would prevent planes from landing. By 1965 the Special Forces had installed rocket launchers and mortars to defend the base against the North Vietnamese and Vietcong that were operating in the area. During the evening of January 3, 1966, North Vietnamese troops attacked the base at Khe Sanh. American troops and ARVN soldiers serving at the base suffered 60 or 70 casualties that resulted from the attack. The Communists usually struck under cover of darkness to avoid being shelled by U.S. bombers, then by the following morning the attack had ended.

As the war expanded, Khe Sanh gradually grew in importance for the U.S. high command. General Westmoreland hoped that some day American troops might launch an assault into Laos to destroy the North

Vietnamese supply routes. Khe Sanh could serve as a base for that invasion. To strengthen Khe Sanh, Navy Seabees were sent to the base to expand and improve the airfield during 1966. That same year, the Special Forces troops were replaced by the Third Marine Division in late September. The marines arrived just in time to experience the full impact of the monsoon season that turned everything to mud and water. Nevertheless, the marines sent out regular patrols to search for Communist troops that were menacing Khe Sanh. The patrols discovered North Vietnamese bunkers, tunnels, and a supply depot. One patrol also withstood a heavy Communist attack, losing some of their men. The other men, however, were rescued by American helicopters that had been called into the area.

In the meantime, the marines worked on Route 9, repairing bridges and improving the road so supplies could reach Khe Sanh more easily. Without this route, the base would be forced to rely entirely on air transport planes to provide food and ammunition for the troops, just as the French had done at Dien Bien Phu. The North Vietnamese, however, continued to threaten Khe Sanh, and a fierce battle broke out on the night of March 15, 1967. One company of the Third Marine Division took heavy casualties and was knocked out of action.

This battle, along with many others that followed in 1967 and 1968, became a titanic struggle between U.S. forces and the Communists for control of the hilly landscape in the Khe Sanh area. The base itself was located on a hill, and around it were other hills that were strategically important to the protection of the base. One of them was called Hill 861, which lay northwest of the base. The battle in March had occurred there. In April, more patrols were sent out to the hill to remove any NVA troops that might be occupying it. Some of the marines searched through caves that might be hiding enemy

U.S. Marines and South Vietnamese troops fought a series of intense battles on the hills of Khe Sanh. Here a helicopter lifts a cannon into position at the top of a hill occupied by the combined forces.

troops. Meanwhile, the marines were attacked by NVA troops on the hillside. When the marines called for support from U.S. aircraft, disaster occurred. As one officer put it: "We got bombed by our jets up there. My squad got six people killed." It would not be the only time that American soldiers would lose their lives, not to the enemy, but to their own "friendly fire." It was extremely difficult for American fighter-bombers to drop their bombs with absolute precision, especially when their own troops were fighting so near the enemy.

After repeated U.S. assaults, however, the Communists were eventually driven off Hill 861 by the end of April. The combination of marine fire power and repeated heavy bombing by U.S. planes proved too much for the NVA defenders. Much of the bombing was carried out by large B-52 bombers in a mission called ARC LIGHT. During the months of battle around Khe Sanh, ARC LIGHT bombers would drop tons and tons of bombs on North Vietnamese positions.

After the fall of Hill 861, the U.S. Marines began an assault on another North Vietnamese position to the west located on Hill 881 South. The marines, under the command of Colonel Gary Wilder, encountered stiff fire from the NVA defending Hill 881 South. The Communists had created emplacements for mortars to fire down on the U.S. troops as they scaled the hillside. With help from marines on nearby Hill 861 and heavy bombing from U.S. planes, American troops finally occupied Hill 881 South by May 2. But American casualties, once again, had been very heavy.

Nevertheless, the marines continued their assaults on the hills surrounding Khe Sanh. Without control of these hills, the enemy might make the main base at Khe Sanh impossible to hold. By May 5, the marines had taken Hill 881 North, which lay farther to the northwest. For the men who fought these battles, however, and saw their fellow soldiers wounded or killed, the hill fights were an experience they would never forget. They struggled against an elusive enemy that knew the terrain far better

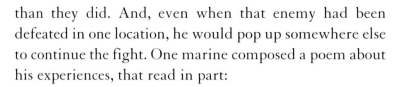

than they did. And, even when that enemy had been defeated in one location, he would pop up somewhere else to continue the fight. One marine composed a poem about his experiences, that read in part:

> My rifle is at the ready, my senses are keener and
>   sharper than they have ever been.
>
> For no squirrel or rabbit will this day grace my game bag.
>
> For today we are after bigger game, game that is
>   wiser and knows the ways of these woods, the
>   hills called Khe Sanh.
>
> They live here, they have lived here for untold thou-
>   sands of years.
>
> These are men of the woods, the woods called Khe Sanh.
>
> We are the intruder, we are the trespasser, we don't belong,
>   not in these hills, these hills called Khe Sanh.

In the spring of 1967, the Third Marine Division was replaced at Khe Sanh by the Twenty-Sixth Marine Division. The base was very busy, as more and more flights came in each day with supplies and ammunition to support the assaults against the surrounding hills. At the base itself, there were rows of trenches to provide protection for the troops. However, some of the key installations at the base were not adequately fortified, such as the ammunition dumps and air traffic control buildings. The marines had been too busy fighting for control of the surrounding hillsides to completely fortify the main base.

Although the Vietnamese had been driven off several of the hills, they had not stopped their activity in the Khe Sanh area. In June, they hit a marine observation post on Hill 950, due north of the base. Eventually, the assault was beaten back and with reinforcements, the marines held their position. In August, the marines received a new commander, Colonel David E. Lownds. He was a veteran of World War II, where he fought against the Japanese in the Pacific. He had also served during the Korean War, but Khe Sanh was his first command in Vietnam. After taking command, Lownds began to notice increasing North Vietnamese interest in Khe Sanh. In September 1967, American intelligence reported that two battalions of North Vietnamese troops, approximately 1,600 men, had been moved into the area. In addition, the amount of supplies had increased along the Ho Chi Minh Trail. In November, North Vietnam moved the famous 304th Division to Khe Sanh. The 304th had led the struggle against the French during the 1950s and participated in the decisive Communist victory at Dien Bien Phu.

Indeed some American political leaders had begun to fear that Khe Sanh might turn into another Dien Bien Phu. The North Vietnamese had successfully closed Route 9, leaving air transport planes as the only means of supplying Khe Sanh. The French had faced a similar situation at Dien Bien Phu. However, the situation at Khe Sanh was quite different. The French position had been in a valley, and the North Vietnamese had controlled the surrounding hills. At Khe Sanh, the U.S. forces occupied much stronger positions. Khe Sanh itself was on a hill and marine positions had also been established at the outlying hill positions around Khe Sanh. In addition, American forces possessed a much stronger air force than the French had been able to use. General Westmoreland was convinced that he could continue to support Khe Sanh completely through the air if it should be heavily attacked.

In January 1968, the possibility of heavy attack seemed to grow closer. On the night of January 2, an advance post beyond the airfield at Khe Sanh spotted six men walking near them. When the marines told the men to stop, they did nothing. The marines began to fire, killing five of the men and wounding the sixth. These men turned out to be high ranking officers in the North Vietnamese army and were apparently on a reconnaissance mission. For these officers to be in the area could only mean that the North Vietnamese were planning a major assault.

For General Westmoreland this was all the proof necessary to confirm his belief that Khe Sanh would be the major battle of the coming Vietnam offensive, which he expected to begin near the lunar new year, Tet. Westmoreland hoped that the North Vietnamese would make a heavy commitment to the assault, then he would hit them with overwhelming U.S. technology and fire power. Westmoreland's plan, called Operation Niagara, began in early January, with intelligence gathering of North Vietnamese positions. U.S. planes took aerial pictures of the Khe Sanh area to detect enemy positions. Helicopters also began to drop sophisticated sensor devices onto the ground to detect troop movements. These included "acoustic sensors to pick up voices; [and] seismic sensors to determine vibrations from marching soldiers, trucks and tanks." Following this phase, Niagara II began, which included heavy air assaults on enemy positions with B-52 bombers as well as more than 3,000 helicopters. Meanwhile, Khe Sanh was reinforced, and the marines sent out frequent patrols to search for suspected North Vietnamese activity.

While General Westmoreland put his plans into operation, the North Vietnamese were reinforcing their own strength around Khe Sanh. In total, Communist forces would number about 22,000, opposed by only about one-third that number of marines. During the afternoon of January 20, a North Vietnamese soldier

U.S. forces used helicopters to drop acoustic and seismic sensors to detect enemy troop movements.

appeared under a flag of truce at Khe Sanh and surrendered. Lieutenant La Thanh Tonc revealed that Communist attacks would begin that night against Hill 861, followed by a major assault against Khe Sanh. Small skirmishes had already occurred on Hill 881 North, but nothing like

North Vietnamese soldiers repeatedly launched major assaults against U.S.-South Vietnamese positions for control of Khe Sanh.

the attacks described by Lieutenant Tonc. The marines were not sure whether to believe Tonc. But then the attacks began, just as he had told them. Following a mortar barrage, "They crept as close to our lines as possible under the cover of supporting arms," one American officer said, "then began to throw sticks of dynamite . . . over the wire to simulate mortars still landing." At another point on Hill 861, recalled a marine, "you could see hundreds and hundreds of NVA coming up our hill, up the slopes. They were yelling, firing." With support from Hill 881, the marines held their position on Hill 861. Colonel Lownds also sent reinforcements to Hill 881. In addition, marines took control of another hill, Hill 861A, which had served as a base for the North Vietnamese attack.

On January 21, the North Vietnamese also began a heavy bombardment of Khe Sanh. One of the first targets to be hit was the exposed ammunition dump. Thousands of shells were lost, and they had to be quickly replaced by air transports so soldiers on Khe Sanh could continue to defend the area. Meanwhile, the Communists overran Khe Sanh village along Route 9, forcing marines to rapidly evacuate, leaving some weapons behind.

Ten days before the Tet Offensive had formally begun, the marines at Khe Sanh found themselves under heavy assault from the North Vietnamese. Historians are unsure whether General Giap, who was in overall command of the Communist offensive, wanted the battle at Khe Sanh to become another Dien Bien Phu. According to another North Vietnamese deserter who gave himself up on January 22, he and his comrades had been told that the fall of Khe Sanh would be the decisive battle of the war. After it fell, the North Vietnamese would advance eastward and capture all of Route 9 and cut off the northern provinces of South Vietnam. But the deserter may only have been fed propaganda by his superiors. It is also possible that Khe Sanh was a diversion meant to distract the U.S. high command from the upcoming Communist attacks against the South Vietnamese cities.

While these attacks were underway, the Communist assault on Khe Sanh continued. On the night of February 3, the American sensors that had been dropped during Operation Niagara detected heavy enemy troop move-ments. It appeared that Hill 861 or Hill 881 would soon be under attack. But the preparations for attack were disrupted by heavy artillery fire from American positions. Then, in the early morning hours of February 5, Hill 861A was attacked. The North Vietnamese came so close that the marines were forced to resort to hand-to-hand combat to beat them back from the hill.

Meanwhile, the North Vietnamese were preparing a major assault against the town of Lang Vei. It was located south of Khe Sanh along Route 9. The marines held a position there to defend the southern flank of the main base. Many of the troops, however, were Laotian soldiers who had fled their homes as well as Vietnamese guerrilla forces that lived in the hills. The total allied force was about 500 troops. Shelling of Lang Vei occurred on February 6. Then, on the following night, the North Vietnamese struck in force. Their attack also included tanks, rarely used by the Communists in South Vietnam. The marines were successful in destroying two of the tanks coming toward them, but other tanks appeared in their rear. It was too much for the marines to withstand, and the North Vietnamese overran the entire camp. At the same time, the Communists were shelling the main base at Khe Sanh to prevent the Americans from providing artillery support for Lang Vei nearby. It was also difficult to land reinforcements at Lang Vei because a helicopter airlift in the dark was extremely dangerous. In addition, marine infantry landed from helicopters would have been no match for the enemy tanks. Some of the marines defending Lang Vei escaped and reached Khe Sanh, but over 200 troops were dead or missing.

While battles were raging in Hue and Saigon, attacks continued against the marine positions at Khe Sanh. One marine detachment had been defending a position at a rock quarry on Hill 64. In the morning darkness of February 8, the North Vietnamese struck this position.

Following a barrage of artillery fire, they attacked the marine bunkers. At first, the marines were overwhelmed, losing almost two-thirds of their force of 65 men. Then the defense stiffened. Corporal Arnold Alderette was wounded but still managed to use his machine gun to drive back the enemy. He was later awarded a Silver Star Medal for his bravery. Eventually, the marine position was reinforced, and the North Vietnamese attackers were driven off.

The key to Khe Sanh was the airfield. If the NVA could have closed it and cut off supplies to the base, they might have won an enormous victory. Although the field was hit repeatedly by Communist mortar and other artillery shells, it was constantly repaired. The repair work was extremely risky because the American soldiers could be hit by sniper fire or mortar attacks. But the repairs continued, allowing the regular flights bringing tons and tons of food supplies and ammunition to support the base. Communist attacks, however, reduced the flights on some days, and the airfield was even closed for repairs during some hours in early February. The planes would then drop supplies by parachute. Meanwhile helicopters supplied the marines on the hill positions outside of Khe Sanh. Nevertheless, the intrepid helicopter pilots had to brave heavy Communist artillery attacks as they landed at the hill positions. However, the American high command wanted to make sure there would be no repeat of Dien Bien Phu.

During February, the bombardments continued. At night, the North Vietnamese were also digging trenches that brought them closer and closer to the perimeter of the main base at Khe Sanh. From these advanced positions, they might be able to launch a powerful assault that could overrun the base before the marines had time to mount a successful defense. From February 21 to 23,

"We Have Been Lucky So Far"

On February 25, 1968, a patrol was sent out under the command of Lieutenant Don Jacques. Consisting of 47 marines, the patrol was supposed to locate a North Vietnamese mortar position that had been creating havoc at Khe Sanh. Before leaving on the patrol, Jacques wrote his sister: "We have been lucky so far and I hope good fortune holds for us. Although my platoon has had 30 wounded since Jan. 21st, none have been too serious." Setting out at 8:00 A.M., Jacques and his men had soon encountered enemy soldiers among the trees. Jacques radioed the base asking if he could take prisoners who might provide some useful intelligence about the Communist positions. He ordered his men to advance against the enemy. Suddenly, the North Vietnamese began firing from their hidden positions, hitting many of the advancing marines. Some of them tried to reach a trench and outflank the enemy, but it was no use. Jacques ordered the rest of the men to retreat. But as he was leading his men back, Jacques was severely wounded and died. Only a few men ever returned to Khe Sanh. The rest were killed or captured. Indeed, their bodies were not recovered because of the intense enemy fire in the area.

the base was hit by a heavy bombardment. Perhaps this was the prelude to a major assault by the enemy from their entrenched positions. Regular patrols were sent out to determine whether the enemy was occupying the trenches in strength. These assignments were very dangerous and often resulted in marine casualties.

Since the situation at Khe Sanh had reached a stalemate, General Westmoreland and his commanders decided to take a risky action in an attempt to drive off the North Vietnamese. Up to this time, the American forces had usually tried to avoid B-52 bombing of enemy positions if they were very close to U.S. lines. There was too much chance that Americans might be killed by "friendly fire." By the end of February, however, the U.S.

The American high command unleashed B-52 bombers in a decisive action at Khe Sanh. The planes were able to drop tons of bombs on enemy strongholds.

high command decided that this was the only way to drive off the enemy from Khe Sanh. Meanwhile intelligence reports had indicated that the Communists were building up their troop strength for one more assault. Beginning at the end of February and continuing into early March, ARC LIGHT, the B-52 assault, hammered the enemy. Although, the Communists continued digging trenches outside Khe Sanh, they were also reducing their troop strength in the area. By mid-March, the threat to Khe Sanh had ended.

Battles with the enemy in the surrounding hills would continue, but the marine position at the main base had held. Khe Sanh was an important American victory.

The last piece of a mural of the late Communist revolutionary Ho Chi Minh is put into place on the former Presidential Palace in Ho Chi Minh City (formerly Saigon) in April 2000. The mural was used as part of the celebration of the 25th anniversary of the end of the war.

The Turning Point

The Tet Offensive had begun on January 30, 1968, and continued until February 24. However, skirmishes occurred around some South Vietnamese cities, including Saigon, for days afterward. And the battle at Khe Sanh did not end until mid-March. Historians are still not sure why the North Vietnamese decided to call off the struggle around Khe Sanh. Perhaps it had never had the major significance that General Westmoreland attached to it. During February, while the siege was still underway, the Communists moved three regiments away from Khe Sanh to the battle around Hue. Apparently, the capture of Hue seemed more important to them. In addition, after the ammunition dump at Khe Sanh had been blown up, the North Vietnamese made no attempt to follow up their advantage and launch a full-scale attack against the base. If their primary intent had been to capture Khe Sanh, this would have been the opportunity to do it. Experts have also pointed out that the North Vietnamese commanders made no attempt to cut off the water supply to Khe Sanh. Soldiers at the base received their water from a stream that ran about 1,500 feet outside the installation. Cutting off the water source would have made the American soldiers even more heavily dependent on supplies from airplanes or helicopters, possibly even too dependent for their needs to be met. Perhaps, as some historians have argued, Khe Sanh was a diversion all along. By attacking the major cities, the Communists hoped to win a huge symbolic victory. They wanted to prove to the people of South Vietnam that they could not depend on the government of Saigon or the American army, even with its huge firing power, to protect them. The Communists also anticipated that the people of South Vietnam, especially the Buddhists who were opposed to the regime in Saigon, might rise up and begin a revolt. Combined with the pressure from the Vietcong and the North Vietnamese army, a revolt might topple the government and lead to an American withdrawal. The North Vietnamese leaders, especially General Giap, believed that they had to do something to break the stalemate. They gambled on an all-out offensive during Tet.

There had been no spontaneous revolt by the South Vietnamese. The Tet Offensive had also inflicted huge casualties on the Communist forces. Estimates ranged from a total of about 45,000 dead out of 85,000 Communists engaged to as high as more than 72,000 Communists dead, according to U.S. military official records. The North Vietnamese had failed to capture or hold on to any of the major objectives that they had attacked. In November 1967, General Westmoreland had claimed that American forces were winning the war in Vietnam. At the end of the Tet Offensive, he believed that

Thousands of homeless South Vietnamese refugees fled their villages and headed to major cities.

U.S. forces had defeated the enemy on the battlefield. On the surface, Westmoreland's evaluation was correct. But underneath, the Tet Offensive told a different story.

Throughout South Vietnam, the devastation had been enormous. Over 14,000 civilians had been killed and another 24,000 seriously wounded. Huge areas had been destroyed, creating more than 600,000 new refugees. They streamed into the cities from the countryside, which had been completely lost to the Communist forces. However, major cities, such as Saigon, could not handle the refugee problem. Camps had to be set up as quickly as possible to deal with the homeless. President Thieu announced that his government would immediately establish centers to distribute food and help refugees rebuild their homes. At first, these efforts seemed to be making progress. However, the government was honeycombed with so much corruption that much of the money designated for the people never reached those who needed it most. This further undermined the credibility of the government that had already lost confidence due to its inability to protect townspeople during the Tet Offensive.

In the meantime, President Thieu hoped to regain the initiative by bolstering the strength of the ARVN. He called up 135,000 soldiers in March. However, the ARVN was an unreliable military force. Although some units had fought bravely during the Tet Offensive, many soldiers had deserted. The ARVN seemed content to let the Americans take responsibility for the most dangerous fighting, while depending on U.S. air power to come to the rescue every time there was a major Communist attack.

Indeed, this very situation was now causing grave concern among American political leaders in Washington. Although Westmoreland had claimed a victory during Tet, he still told the Joint Chiefs of Staff, that he needed reinforcements not only to replace his losses during Tet, but also to deal with the growing power of the North Vietnamese throughout South Vietnam. If Tet had really been a military defeat for the Communists, they still had no plans to give up their attempts to take over the South Vietnamese government. In fact, they were sending in more soldiers to fill the ranks that had been reduced during Tet.

As General Westmoreland assessed the situation, he became convinced that a huge increase in the number of American troops would be necessary to win the war in Vietnam. The Joint Chiefs believed that American forces around the world were already stretched too thin. Instead, they wanted President Johnson to begin calling up the reserves in the United States to provide the additional forces. Johnson, however, was not prepared to take this action. Instead, he sent an additional 10,500 troops to South Vietnam.

During the last week of February, the president also dispatched General Earl Wheeler, the chairman of the Joint Chiefs, on a fact-finding mission to South Vietnam. Wheeler's report to President Johnson was filled with bad news. As he told the president: "There is no doubt that the enemy launched a major, powerful nationwide assault. This offensive has by no means run its course." In fact, the battle for Khe Sanh was still underway. Wheeler went on to point out that the ARVN had suffered huge losses, and the Communists were largely in control of the countryside. Wheeler added that Tet "was a very near thing. . . . We suffered a loss, there can be no doubt about it." Wheeler brought home a request from Westmoreland for over 200,000 more troops for South Vietnam.

President Johnson was stunned by the request for such an enormous increase in troop strength. The president asked his newly appointed Secretary of Defense Clark Clifford to evaluate the situation in South Vietnam and come back with his recommendations. Clifford's group advised the president to send approximately 20,000 additional troops but suggested that any huge troop increase be avoided. There would be "no end in sight," the report cautioned. In mid-March, President Johnson convened a meeting of top experts in foreign affairs, known as "the wise men." In the past, they had supported the American involvement in South Vietnam. At this meeting, however, they advised the president that the time had come for the United States to begin reducing its role in South Vietnam. It was clear that no victory was possible.

Nationally known broadcast journalist Walter Cronkite is shown reporting from a bombed out area on the Vietnam war front.

The Tet Offensive, although it had been a military defeat for the Communists, had shown America's political leaders that they must begin disengaging in South Vietnam. The United States press had already begun to recognize that American military power could not win a victory. In February, during the Tet Offensive, Walter Cronkite, who was considered the leading newsman in the United States, visited the war front. He interviewed soldiers in Hue and based on his findings concluded that victory was not possible. Cronkite told Americans that the war had reached a "stalemate" and America should begin to "negotiate, not as victors, but as an honorable people who had lived up to their pledge to defend democracy, and did the best they could."

In the meantime, the political situation was deteriorating at home. During March, Senator Eugene McCarthy had almost won the Democratic primary in New Hampshire, embarrassing President Johnson. Senator Robert Kennedy had decided, as a result of Tet and the president's low ratings in the polls, to enter the race for the Democratic presidential nomination in 1968. Other influential senators had also begun to oppose the war. In addition, the American economy was experiencing serious problems. The cost of running the war in Vietnam and financing the programs of President Johnson's Great Society were more than the United States could afford. On March 31, 1968, President Johnson addressed the nation. He announced a partial halt to the bombing of North Vietnam. Then he added: "We ask that talks begin promptly, that they be serious talks on the substance of peace. . . . We are reducing—substantially reducing—the present level of hostilities. And we are doing so unilaterally, and at once. . . . Now, as in the past," the president continued, "the United States is ready to send its representatives to any forum, at any time, to discuss the means of bringing this ugly war to an end." At the end of his speech, the president said that he would not seek another term as president so he could devote himself to the peace process.

The president's speech, which had been prompted by the Tet Offensive, marked the beginning of the end of American involvement in South Vietnam. Over the next two months, U.S. and North Vietnamese negotiators haggled over a place to hold the peace talks. Eventually, they were convened in Paris in May 1968. In the meantime, the ground war continued in South Vietnam. The ARVN was unable to reassert any control in the countryside. Indeed, the Communists still threatened the major cities in the south. During May, there were renewed attacks by the

North Vietnamese troops against Saigon. The assault began on May 5, and heavy fighting raged in parts of Saigon, including the vital Tan Son Nhut Airport. The Communists were initially pushed back, then 48 hours later, they launched a new attack. Gradually, the Communists were driven out of the city. But several weeks later, the attacks on Saigon continued.

In the north, U.S. activity continued around Khe Sanh. In April, American forces had launched Operation Pegasus, which succeeded in reopening Route 9 as a supply network. But by June, the American high command had apparently reversed itself on the importance of Khe Sanh to the defense of South Vietnam. On June 17, marine units began to take down the base and evacuate the area. Khe Sanh no longer seemed so important, as the Communists continued to focus their attention on major urban areas throughout South Vietnam. However, the American press criticized the decision to evacuate the base at Khe Sanh, especially after the number of casualties that had been sustained there. According to one estimate, over 700 U.S. soldiers had been killed, and more than 2,600 wounded. The enemy had lost even more—10,000 to 13,000 killed or seriously wounded.

While American forces were pulling back, a bitter election contest was being fought in the United States. Amid increasing war protests throughout the country, the Democrats nominated Vice President Hubert Humphrey for president at their convention in Chicago. In Miami, the Republicans nominated former Vice President Richard Nixon. In November, Nixon was elected president in a close election. Following his inauguration in January 1969, the president began to implement a new policy in South Vietnam. Called Vietnamization, it included improved training for the AVN troops of President Thieu, while U.S. involvement in the war started to decline.

In July 1969, American troops began to leave South

These North Vietnamese soldiers were photographed by Dinh Quang Thanh outside of the Presidential Palace in Saigon on April 30, 1975. The North Vietnamese photographer captured this image on the day the war ended.

Vietnam. The troop withdrawal continued until all U.S. ground soldiers had left by early 1973. Two years later, South Vietnam was under the control of the North. Once again all of Vietnam was united, this time under a Communist regime. Saigon was renamed Ho Chi Minh City. The steps leading to the American withdrawal and final Communist victory had started with the Tet Offensive, the turning point of the Vietnam War. Ironically, North Vietnam lost the battles, but won the war.

c. 100 B.C.	Chinese conquer Vietnam and rule for 1,000 years. They introduce Confucianism in Vietnam and bring Buddhism to the country.
938 A.D.	Vietnamese throw off Chinese rule, maintain independence for 1,000 years.
1426	Vietnamese defeat attempt by the Chinese to reconquer country.
1802	Vietnamese establish a single, unified kingdom.
1859	French conquer Saigon.
1873	French conquer Hanoi.
1907	Vietnamese stage unsuccessful revolt against French.
1941	Japanese take control of Vietnam. Vietminh established.
1945	Japan surrenders, ending World War II. Ho Chi Minh declares Vietnam independent on September 2. French reassert control.

1965
American advisers attacked in Pleiku. Johnson begins sending marines to South Vietnam.

1966
383,000 American troops in Vietnam by end of year. Protests against the war are held in United States.

1967
Americans initiate Operation Rolling Thunder to bomb Ho Chi Minh Trail. Marines take control of hills around Khe Sanh.

1964
General Westmoreland becomes commander of U.S. forces in Vietnam. Congress passes Gulf of Tonkin Resolution. President Johnson elected to a full term as president.

1964   1967

Timeline

1954	Communists defeat French at Dien Bien Phu. Vietnam is divided between north and south.
1962	Green Berets occupy Khe Sanh.
1963	South Vietnamese President Ngo Dinh Diem overthrown. President John F. Kennedy assassinated. Vice President Lyndon Johnson becomes president.
1964	General Westmoreland becomes commander of U.S. forces in Vietnam. Congress passes Gulf of Tonkin Resolution. President Johnson elected to a full term as president.
1965	President Johnson launches Great Society programs. American advisers attacked in Pleiku. Johnson begins sending marines to South Vietnam.
1966	383,000 American troops in Vietnam by end of year. Protests against the war are held in United States.

January 30
Communists launch Tet Offensive. Hue, Pleiku, and many other cities are attacked.

January 31
Saigon attacked. Communist forces take control of Hue and attack main citadel.

June 17
Khe Sanh is abandoned by American forces.

1975
Communists take control of South Vietnam.

January 21
Communist attacks begin on marine base at Khe Sanh

February 7
Lang Vei falls to North Vietnamese troops.

November
Richard Nixon elected president.

1968

1975

February 10
Allied forces retake Saigon.

March 31
President Johnson says he will not seek reelection. President calls for partial bombing halt of North Vietnam and urges peace talks

1973
All U.S. ground forces leave Vietnam.

February 24
Allies retake Hue. Tet Offensive ends.

Mid-March
Communist threat to Khe Sanh ends.

1969
America begins to withdraw troops from South Vietnam.

1967	Rev. Martin Luther King denounces Vietnam War. Many Americans oppose American involvement in war. Americans initiate Operation Rolling Thunder to bomb Ho Chi Minh Trail. Marines take control of hills around Khe Sanh.
1968	
January 21	Communist attacks begin on marine base at Khe Sanh
January 30	Communists launch Tet Offensive. Hue, Pleiku, and many other cities are attacked.
January 31	Saigon attacked. Communist forces take control of Hue and attack main citadel.
February 7	Lang Vei falls to North Vietnamese troops.
February 10	Allied forces retake Saigon.
February 24	Allies retake Hue. Tet Offensive ends.
Mid-March	Communist threat to Khe Sanh ends.
March 31	President Johnson says he will not seek reelection. President calls for partial bombing halt of North Vietnam and urges peace talks
June 17	Khe Sanh is abandoned by American forces.
November	Richard Nixon elected president.
1969	America begins to withdraw troops from South Vietnam.
1973	All U.S. ground forces leave Vietnam.
1975	Communists take control of South Vietnam.

Burke, Tracey and Gleason, Mimi. *The Tet Offensive: January—April, 1968.* New York: Gallery Books, 1988.

Dougan, Clark and Weiss, Stephen. *The Vietnam Experience: Nineteen Sixty Eight*, Boston: Boston Publishing Company, 1983.

Doyle, Edward and Lipsman, Samuel. *The Vietnam Experience: Setting the Stage.* Boston: Boston Publishing Company, 1981.

Gilbert, Marc Jason and Head, William, eds. *The Tet Offensive.* Westport, CT: Praeger, 1996.

Hallek, Robert. *Flawed Giant: Lyndon Johnson and His Times, 1961-1973.* New York: Oxford University Press, 1998.

Karnow, Stanley. *Vietnam: A History.* New York: Viking, 1983.

Morrison, Wilbur. *The Elephant and the Tiger: The Full Story of the Vietnam War.* New York: Hippocrene Books, 1990.

Nolan, Keith. *Battle for Hue, Tet, 1968.* Novato, CA: Presidio, 1983.

O'Nan, Stewart, ed. *The Vietnam Reader.* New York: Doubleday, 1998.

Prados, John and Stubbe, Ray. *Valley of Decision: The Siege of Khe Sanh.* Boston: Houghton Mifflin, 1991.

Rice, Earle. *The Tet Offensive.* San Diego: Lucent Books, 1997.

Young, Marilyn. *The Vietnam Wars, 1945-1990.* New York: HarperCollins, 1991.

page:
2:   reprinted from "Vietnam: A
     History," Stanley Karnow
6:   Associated Press, AP
10: Associated Press, AP
13: Corbis
20: Hulton Archive by Getty Images
23: Bettmann/Corbis
24: Associated Press, AP
26: Hulton Archive by Getty Images
29: Associated Press, AP
31: Associated Press, AP
33: Bettmann/Corbis
38: Hulton Archive by Getty Images
43: Associated Press, AP

45: Bettmann/Corbis
48: Bettmann/Corbis
51: Associated Press, AP
54: Bettmann/Corbis
59: Bettmann/Corbis
62: Associated Press, AP
66: Associated Press, AP
72: Associated Press, AP
74: Hulton Archive by Getty Images
77: Associated Press, AP
78: Associated Press, AP
81: © Tim Page/Corbis
84: Hulton Archive by Getty Images
87: Associated Press, AP

cover: © Bettmann/Corbis

frontis: Reprinted from *Vietnam: A History*, Stanley Karnow

RICHARD WORTH has thirty years experience as a writer, trainer, and video producer. He has written more than 25 books, including *The Four Levers of Corporate Change*, a best-selling business book. Many of his books are for young adults on topics that include family living, foreign affairs, biography, history, and the criminal justice system.